I0177751

No More a Secret

Merle M. Mills

No More a Secret

Poems, Prayers, and Promises:
A Guide to Healing After Abortion

Merle M. Mills

Copyright © 2011, 2020 by Merle M. Mills

All rights reserved. No portion of this book may be reproduced, stored in a retrieval system, or transmitted in any form or by any means—electronic, mechanical, photocopy, recording, scanning or other—except for brief quotations in critical reviews or articles, without the prior written permission of the publisher.

Unless otherwise indicated, all Scripture quotations are taken from the Holy Bible, New Living Translation copyright © 1996, 2004, 2007 by Tyndale House Foundation. Used by permission of Tyndale House Publishers, Inc., Carol Stream, Illinois 60188. All rights reserved.

Artwork by Bill Osborne

Content Design by Evelyn J. Wagoner

Published by Easter Press, Fort Myers, Florida

Dedication

I dedicate this book . . . To my unborn child,
A day never ends without my having
thought about you.
My heart still aches, because I miss you.

To those women who hurt silently,
I have bared and opened my heart
so that you may know
the hope and comfort that I have come to know.

To my family . . .
without knowing, you nurtured me
from brokenness to wholeness.

To women
faced with the decision whether to abort,
avoid making a rushed decision. Seek wise counsel.
Think. And after thinking … think again!

To my God,
Thank You for loving me.
Most of all, thank You for forgiving me.

Contents

God's Promises for:

Poems & Prayers

"For I am persuaded that neither death, nor life, nor angels, nor principalities, nor powers, nor things present, nor things to come, nor height, nor depth, nor any other creature, shall be able to separate us from the love of God, which is in Christ Jesus our Lord."

Romans 8:38-39 (KJV)

Questions

Lord,
why would You love
someone like me?
Why do I deserve
Your love?
I don't understand.
Why, Lord?
Why would You
forgive
someone like me?
Why, Lord?

My child,
did not I say
I will forgive all your sin?
Did not I say
My love is everlasting?
Nothing
can ever separate you
from My love,
from My forgiveness.
I have forgiven you.
I love you.
Will you believe it?
Will you accept it?

Father, my questions are always the same: Do I deserve Your love? Your forgiveness? Do You really understand what I have done?

Daughter, My answer to you is always the same: My love for you is everlasting. I have forgiven you. Nothing can ever separate you from My love, not even abortion. Ask, then believe it. Accept it. It is My gift to you!

"And I heard a great voice out of heaven saying. Behold the tabernacle of God is with men and He will dwell with them, and they shall be His people, and God Himself shall be with them, and be their God. And God shall wipe away all tears from their eyes, and there shall be no more death, neither sorrow, nor crying, neither shall there be any more pain, for the former things are passed away."

Revelation 21:3-4 (KJV)

tears

When I think about
never touching
you,
never knowing
you,
saying goodbye
before
saying hello,
tears come.
Then I think
of Heaven
touching
you,
holding
you,
knowing
you,
saying hello,
never
saying goodbye
again
tears
are wiped
away.

Father, there are times when I think about missing the tender touch of my child, and I begin to shed tears. Somehow my tears do not satisfy the deep sadness, the longing, and the loneliness in my heart.

Dear daughter, I feel your hurt. I feel your pain. Heaven is real. Your child is with Me. Live your life to ensure that one day you will be here with Me and your child. Then your heart will never be lonely again.

"The Spirit of the Lord is upon Me, because He hath anointed Me to preach the gospel to the poor; He hath sent Me to heal the brokenhearted, to preach deliverance to the captives, and recovering of sight to the blind, to set at liberty them that are bruised."

Luke 4:18 (KJV)

No More a Secret

It used to be a secret,
   my child,
That I didn't give you
    a name
    a home

It used to be a secret
   how my heart
   would cry out
   in shame

It used to be a secret
   my tears
   my pain

Now
It's no more a secret
   that I threw myself
   overwhelmed
   with grief
   at the Savior's feet

Oh, my God
set me free
from this secret

Now
It's no more a secret
that He did!

Father, for years, shame, guilt, depression, and grief overwhelmed me. Sometimes, it still does, and the pain is too much to bear.

Precious daughter, My promises to you are all true. I want to heal your broken heart. I want to set you free from the after-pain of aborting your child. I want you to experience My love, My forgiveness. I want you to live the abundant life that I offer you, free from shame, free from guilt, free from depression, free from grief. Come to Me. I will give you My peace.

"And their sins and iniquities I will remember no more."

Hebrews 10:17 (KJV)

Will You Remind Me?

Father
there are
still times
when
i am reminded
of
the pain
the shame
the loneliness
and i shed
secret tears

during those times
will You
remind me
to look into
Your face
to touch

Your hands
Your side
Your feet?

during those times
will You
remind me
that
You love me
and that
You have
forgiven me?

Father, there are times when I cannot help but remember the shame, the pain, the emptiness, the void left in my life without my child. During these times, I need You to remind me that You love me and that You have forgiven me.

Daughter, let My blood-stained face, My pierced hands. . . My side. . . My feet, always be your greatest reminder that I love you, and that I have forgiven you.

"I love You Lord; You are my strength. The Lord is my rock, my fortress, and my Savior; my God is my rock in whom I find protection. He is my shield, the power that saves me, and my place of safety. I called on the Lord, who is worthy of praise, and He saved me from my enemies."

Psalm 18:1-3

In Your Presence

These are the moments
I treasure most
when I am in Your presence
and
You see me
as I am
frail
broken
and
with Your touch of love
You
strengthen me
You
calm my doubts and fears
with Your touch of love
You open my eyes
and
I see You
as You are
my hope
my future
my all.

Father, my emotions are frail . . . broken. I need Your presence to give me hope. Help me understand that only Your love has the power to heal, strengthen, and calm my doubts and fears.

My daughter, I am delighted when you accept My offer to heal and restore your broken heart. Let Me be your hope. Let Me be your future. Let Me be your all.

Jesus prayed to the Father: "that they also may be one in Us; that the world may believe that You have sent Me."

John 17:21b (KJV)

Wrapped

I unwrapped my heart before Him
    a heart
    broken
    torn
    each beat
    filled
    with sorrow
    each beat
    filled
    with pain.

I wept as He wrapped
    each beat
    with forgiveness
    each beat
    with love
    two hearts
    wrapped together
    now beating
    as
    one.

Father, I give you my heart. It's broken. It's filled with pain. It's filled with sorrow. It is impossible for me to go on with it beating this way.

Dearest daughter, give Me your broken heart. Read My promises to forgive you, to love you, and to heal your broken heart often. Memorize them. Let them be your companion. Let them be constantly in your thoughts, and our hearts will be wrapped as one. Remember, My daughter, My love for you is endless.

"Don't be afraid, for I am with you. Don't be discouraged; for I am your God. I will strengthen you and help you. I will hold you up with my victorious right hand."

Isaiah 41:10

To You from me

my helper
my friend
my peace
i adore
You

for hope
for joy
for forgiveness
i thank
You

for transforming
my yesterdays
my todays
my tomorrows
from weakness
to strength
i love
You

Father, from my heart, I give You thanks and adoration for transforming my life. I shall be eternally grateful.

Dear daughter, My desire is that you understand, it is not a secret that you are the apple of My eye. I have forgiven you. You are precious in My sight. You are valuable to Me. I love you.

7 Do's That Helped Me Heal

Do acknowledge sin and
ask God
for forgiveness.

One definition of sin in Webster's Dictionary is the breaking of a law of God.

Destroying human life breaks the law of God. I had broken this law, and along with Psalm 51, confessed, *"Against You and You alone have I sinned . . . because of Your great compassion . . . wash me clean from my guilt. Purify me from my sin."*

Do seek counseling.

Since I was so ashamed of aborting my child, I made a vow never to share my experience with anyone. For years, I did not. I finally realized that I could not go on living with the pain, the anger, the guilt, the depression, and the shame that had secretly controlled me.

Many churches and counseling services nationwide offer specialized counseling. I chose to attend a confidential abortion support recovery group offered by the Crisis Pregnancy Center of Tidewater. Through the caring atmosphere and God's tender mercy, I received extensive healing, restoration, and freedom.

Do make a commitment to begin each day with prayer.

In prayer, I learned that my Heavenly Father said, *"I will answer them before they even call to Me. While they are still talking about their needs, I will go ahead and answer their prayers!"* (Isaiah 65:24)

I am learning that I can trust Him and that, through expressing my innermost feelings in prayer, He provides the comfort I desperately need.

Do make a commitment to daily Bible study.

In the Holy Scriptures, there are answers and solutions for all the challenges we face in life. I established and still maintain a personal study schedule. During this time, I especially focus on and memorize God's promises for healing my broken heart, promises of His offer to forgive me, and promises that nothing I have done could ever separate me from His extravagant love.

Do keep a journal.

Keeping a journal affords me the opportunity to look back over my life and compare where I was to where I am today. It demonstrates how God's power has transformed my life from pain to peace . . . depression to joy . . . weakness to strength.

Do allow yourself

to grieve.

In her book, *Forgiven & Set Free*, Linda Cochrane writes: "Depression may also result from feelings of sorrow and grief that go unrelieved because there is no place in our society to mourn the loss of an aborted child." One definition of grief is: "deep sadness or mental distress caused by a loss."

More and more each day, it became evident—I had experienced a great loss—the loss of my child. Grieving allowed me to express the "deep sadness and mental distress," which resulted from that devastating loss.

Do be patient with yourself during the healing process.

Memories of the abortion experience do not go away. There are still days when they seem more vivid, and I have doubts of my healing journey. On these days, when my feelings are like the weather, one day overcast . . . one day sunny, I remind myself that my trust is in a God who is changeless, and whose promises for forgiving me and loving me remain steadfast.

God's Promises

The following Scriptures helped me understand and receive healing for feelings of shame, regret, guilt, depression, hopelessness, and the need to be forgiven and accepted. As you read them, my prayer is that you will open your heart and let them personally speak to your life.

Shame

In thee, O Lord, do I put my trust. Let me never be ashamed.[1] The one who believes in Him will never be ashamed.[2]

For the Lord your God is living among you. He is a mighty Savior. He will take delight in you with gladness. With His love He will calm all your fears. He will rejoice over you with joyful songs.[3]

Instead of shame and dishonor, you will possess a double portion of prosperity . . . and everlasting joy will be yours.[4]

And My people shall never be ashamed.[5]

[1]Psalm 31:1 (KJV)
[2]Romans 9:33 (ISV)
[3]Zephaniah 3:17
[4]Isaiah 61:7
[5]Joel 2:27b (KJV)

Regret

I focus on this one thing: forgetting the past and looking at what lies ahead.[1] For I am about to do something new. See, I have already begun! Do you not see it?[2] Great is His faithfulness; His mercies begin afresh each morning.[3] This means that anyone who belongs to Christ has become a new person. The old life is gone; a new life has begun.[4]

He has given me a new song to sing, a hymn of praise to our God. Many will see what He has done and be amazed.[5]

[1] Philippians 3:13
[2] Isaiah 43:19a
[3] Lamentations 3:23
[4] 11 Corinthians 5:17
[5] Psalms 40:3a

Guilt

For God sent not His Son into the world to condemn the world, but that the world through Him might be saved.[1] And Jesus said unto her, *"Neither do I condemn you, go and sin no more."*[2]

Finally, I confessed all my sins to You and stopped trying to hide my guilt . . . and You forgave me! All my guilt is gone.[3]

God is faithful and reliable. If we confess our sins, He forgives them and cleanses us from everything we've done wrong.[4]

Come now, let's settle this, says the LORD. Though your sins are like scarlet, I will make them as white as snow. Though they are red like crimson, I will make them as white as wool.[5]

[1] John 3:17 (KJV)
[2] John 8:11 (KJV)
[3] Psalms 32:5
[4] 1 John 1:9 (GWT)
[5] Isaiah 1:18

Depression

From the ends of the earth, I cry to You when my heart is overwhelmed. Lead me to the towering rock of safety.[1] When I am afraid, I will put my trust in You.[2] You will keep in perfect peace all who trust in You, all those whose thoughts are fixed on You![3] You have turned my mourning into joyful dancing. You have taken away my clothes of mourning and clothed me with joy.[4]

I will turn their mourning into joy. I will comfort them and exchange their sorrow for rejoicing.[5]

[1]Psalms 61:2
[2]Psalm 56:3
[3]Isaiah 26:3
[4]Psalm 30:11
[5]Jeremiah 31:13b

Hopelessness

For in Thee, O Lord, do I hope; Thou will hear, O Lord my God.[1] And I am certain that God, who began the good work within you, will continue His work until it is finally finished on the day when Christ Jesus returns.[2]

The Lord will be the hope of His people.[3] And so, Lord, where do I put my hope? My only hope is in You.[4] Why am I so discouraged? Why is my heart so sad? I will put my hope In God! I will praise Him again —my Savior and my God![5]

[1]Psalm 38:15 (KJV)
[2]Philippians: 1:6
[3]Joel 3:16b (KJV)
[4]Psalm 39:7
[5]Psalm 43:5

Forgiveness

Where is another God like You, who pardons the guilt of the remnant, overlooking the sins of His special people? You will not stay angry with Your people forever, because You delight in sowing unfailing love. Once again You will have compassion on us. You will trample our sins under Your feet and throw them into the depths of the ocean![1] But You offer forgiveness that we might learn to fear You.[2] He forgives all my sins and heals all my diseases.[3]

I—yes, I alone—will blot out your sins for My own sake and will never think of them again.[4] And I will forgive their wickedness, and I will never again remember their sins.[5]

O Lord, You are so good, so ready to forgive, so full of unfailing love for all who ask for Your help.[6]

[1]Micah 7:18-19
[2]Psalm 130:4
[3]Psalm 103:3
[4]Isaiah 43:25
[5]Hebrews 8:12b
[6]Psalms 86:5

Acceptance

Keep me as the apple of Your eye; hide me in the shadow of Your wings.[1] And the very hairs of your head are all numbered.[2] How precious are Your thoughts about me, O God. They cannot be numbered. I can't even count them; they outnumber the grains of sand.[3]

I have called you by name, you are Mine[4]. . . so don't be afraid; you are more valuable to *Me* than a whole flock of sparrows.[5] I have loved you with an everlasting love. With unfailing love I have drawn you to Myself.[6] You are precious to Me. You are honored, and I love you.[7]

[1]Psalm 17:8 (NIV)
[2]Matthew 10:30
[3]Psalm 139:17-18
[4]Isaiah 43:1c
[5]Matthew 10:31
[6]Jeremiah 31:3c
[7]Isaiah 43:4b

Heaven's Joy

empty arms
silent cries
your voice
never heard

my love
suspended
awaiting
the dawn

when
holding you
will heal
hidden teardrops

when
holding you
will heal
shattered moments

then
knowing you
since
i never knew you
will be
joy
such joy
heaven's joy
forever
and
ever
and
ever.

My Prayer for You!

I pray that you will accept His gift of peace[1] and that you will not let your heart be troubled.[2]

I pray that you will give all your worries and cares to Him, because He cares about what happens to you.[3]

I pray that you will forget the failures and disappointments of the past, forget those things that are behind, and reach forward to those things that are ahead.[4]

I pray that you will receive His forgiveness, because He has promised to forgive all our iniquities,[5] and remember them no more.[6]

I pray, that you will know that He loves you with an everlasting love,[7] and that you will be convinced that neither death, nor life, nor angels, nor principalities, nor things present, nor things to come, nor height, nor depth, nor any other created thing shall be able to separate you from the love of God which is in Christ Jesus our Lord.[8] Amen!

[1]John 14:27; [2]John 14:1a; [3]1 Peter 5:7; [4]Philippians 3:13b; [5]Psalm 103:3; [6]Hebrews 10:17; [7]Jeremiah 31:3b; [8]Romans 8:38-39

A Plea
from the Unborn

Do you know that I am a gift from the Lord,[1] and that He knew me before He formed me in your womb?[2] Did you know He made all the delicate, inner parts of my body and knit me together,[3] and it is a mystery how I am formed in your womb?[4] Do you know that His Spirit made me and His Almighty breath gave me life[5] and that I am a gift and a reward from Him?[6]

Will you preserve my life?

[1]Psalm 127a
[2]Jeremiah 1:5a
[3]Psalm 139:13
[4]Ecclesiastes 11:5b
[5]Job 33:4
[6]Psalm 127:3

No More a Secret

is the healing journey that transformed my hurting life to peace . . . to joy . . . to strength.

My prayer is that, as you join me in your journey to healing, you too will experience God's extravagant, unconditional love and His unlimited promises to forgive our sin.

Merle M. Mills

Changedthrutheword.org

An Invitation

If, after reading this book, you would like to have a personal relationship with Jesus Christ, the One who promises to offer healing, forgiveness, and peace after abortion, following is a prayer you can pray:

Father, You have promised that if I confess my sin, You will forgive my sin and cleanse me from all wrong that I have done (1John 1:9). I accept Your forgiveness and cleansing. Take my hand and walk with me for the rest of my life. In Jesus' name, amen.

About the Author

Merle's extensive search for peace and wholeness after abortion led to the pages of the Holy Scriptures. There she discovered promises, offering forgiveness from the past, and hope for her future. *No More A Secret* was birthed on the discovery of this newfound hope.

As a writer/speaker, she unashamedly shares her testimony of a journey from pain to peace, depression to joy, and weakness to strength. Her prayer is that her audience will allow the power of the ever-living God the freedom to do the same in and through their lives.

Special Thanks

To Evelyn J. Wagoner for the many hours spent in editing, encouragement, and enthusiasm to support the dream.

To the KPC Writers Group, you helped me discover the gift of writing that God has placed in me.

EASTER PRESS

Easter Press is the first outreach of a much larger vision of the Gospel Commune. Our purpose is to assist Christian authors in getting their books into the hands of those who need them.

> *"My heartfelt gratitude goes to Bill and Joanna with Easter Press for their support. They were sent to me at a time when it was most critical for the production of my book."*
>
> Jack Spiers, Author
> *I'll Ride My White Horse Again*

Our goal is to remove the financial and technical hurdles which have traditionally hindered new Christian authors from becoming published and spreading the Gospel of Jesus Christ.

If you have a manuscript which you would like to submit for consideration, please visit our website at www.EasterPress.com.

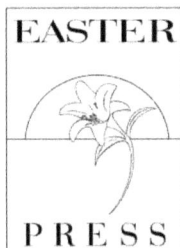

EASTER

PRESS

"...We are the Easter people and hallelujah is our song."
- Pope John Paul II

www.ingramcontent.com/pod-product-compliance
Lightning Source LLC
Chambersburg PA
CBHW071637040426
42452CB00009B/1660

* 9 7 8 0 9 8 8 6 1 6 2 4 0 *